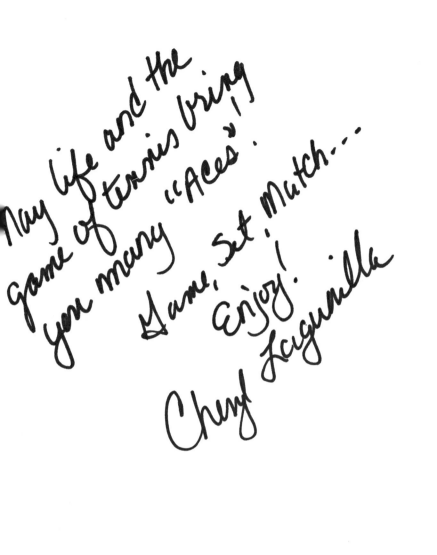

May life and the
game of tennis bring
you many "Aces".

Game. Set. Match...
Enjoy!
Cheryl Laguinilla

The ABC's Of Tennis

By Cheryl Lagunilla

Illustrated by James Himsworth 3

GHL Publishing, LLC • Pennsylvania, USA

Aa is for Aces

served up hard
and fast.

Balls
hit at Angles
fly right on past.

Bb is for

Bounce.
Shout it loud
and clear,

when Balls hit with

Backhands

are way out

of here.

C c is for Courts

where you

play and Compete, and a Coach who reminds you to run with fast feet.

Dd is for Drills

on Defense and Drop shots.

Playing Doubles with friends, the fun never stops.

Ee is for Everyone.

Everyone can play!

"Keep your Eye on the ball," is all I can say.

Ff is for Friends.

Playing tennis
only takes two.
You'll have Fun with

Forehands, Footwork and Follow through.

Gg is for
"Good   Gets"
and Ground strokes
played by you
and by me.

Games played on

Grass courts are so

fun to see.

Hh is for

Hard courts where the game can take place,

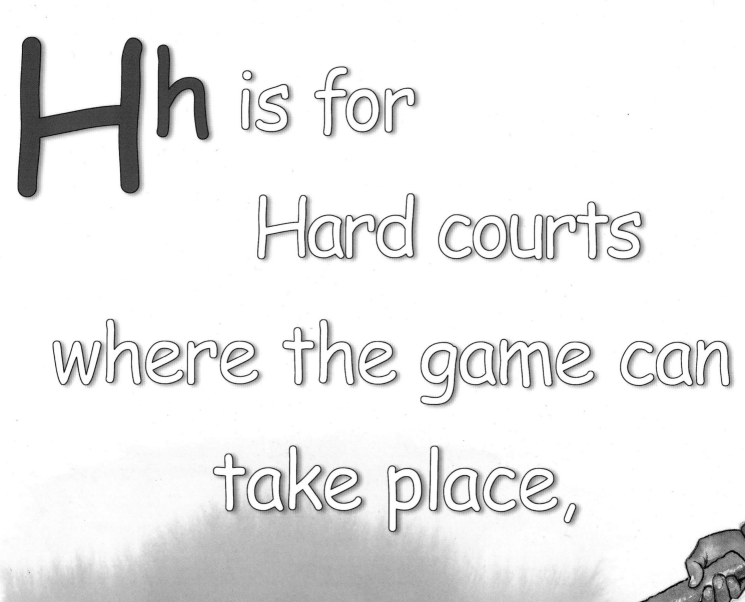

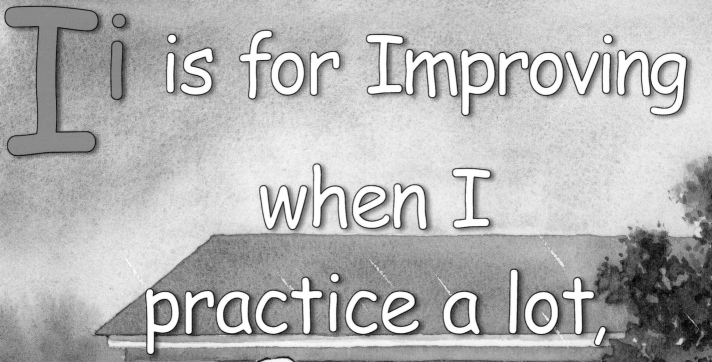

I i is for Improving

when I practice a lot,

Indoors and outdoors,

perfecting

my shots.

Jj is for

Junior league

where
I hope to compete.

Teamwork
and friendship
          really sound
              neat.

Kk is for all Kids girls and boys, young and old.

This game will last a lifetime and reward you tenfold.

L l is for Love. No player wants to be there.

It's as bad as a Line call

that just isn't fair.

Mm is for Marathon Matches lasting 3 to 5 sets.

SET	1	2	3	4	5
RED →	6	7	4	3	4
BLUE →	4	5	6	6	5

It's important

at Match point
to play at your best.

Nn is for Net

which

my shots

have to clear

and Never
giving up when

victory is Near.

These
Offensive shots
are sure
hard to beat.

Pp is for Practice
and Patience

needed to learn all these things.

Just think of
the joy

a great
Passing shot brings.

Qq is for Quickly. that's how points are played out.

Quietly you watch.

Shhhh....
Please do not shout.

Rr is for Racquets set in

Ready position.

Good returns

come after

much repetition.

Ss is for Strokes
hit with Slices and Spins.

I'm hoping
the Score
in this Set
shows I win.

Tt is for a Tiebreaker

I must win in this set.

GAME SCORE

BLUE	6	5	6		
RED	4	7	6		

A great Toss
and good Timing
would be
a sure bet.

Uu is for Universal.
That's what
this game has become.

Vv is for Volleys

where good Vision

is best

and
Victories
hard won
that put you
to the test.

Ww is for Warm-ups and Workouts, necessary parts of this game.

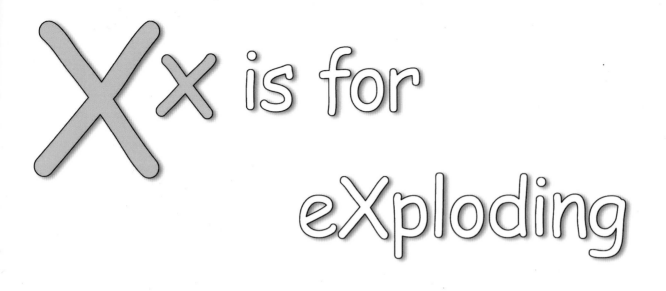

Xx is for eXploding as you step toward the ball.

EXpecting to win is eXciting, but have fun above all.

Yy is for You, the most important part of this rhyme.

You and your family come together to have a good time.

Zz is for Zones where balls are hit to just the right spots

and the Zip

and the Zeal

it takes

to execute shots.

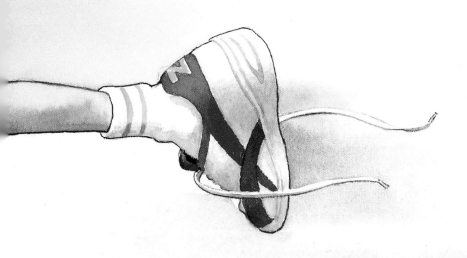

Learning your ABC's is fun.
Yet we feel our work here
has just begun.

Bringing tennis to families
is what we hope to do.
A lifetime of good memories
is just waiting for you.

To the "Aces" of our life – Mark, Annie, Michael and Elizabeth.
Love, your biggest fans, Mom and Dad

To our pride and joy – Zane, Brady and Annie.
Love, Mom and Dad

To our two favorite tennis players – David and John. Thank you
for your ideas and inspiration during the writing of this book.
Never lose your passion for life! You are awesome!
Love, Mom and Dad

The ABC's of Tennis

Text © 2003 by GHL Publishing LLC
Illustrations © 2003 by James Himsworth 3
The illustrations in this book were rendered in watercolor

Edited by Mark Himsworth.
Mark Gama – What a great idea!

Printed in Korea.

Book design by JohnnyHighRez

Lagunilla, Cheryl N.
The ABC's of Tennis/by Cheryl N. Lagunilla; illustrated by James Himsworth 3
Summary: Learning your ABC's can be fun when you join some active and
enthusiastic kids who demonstrate tennis using the letters of the alphabet.

Library of Congress # 2002095970

ISBN: 0-9726419-0-4

SAN #254-9875
Distributed in USA by GHL Publishing LLC
P.O. Box 26462
Collegeville, PA 19426
www.GHLPublishing.com